MW01124596

nothing memorable stays the same

a book of poems by kyle fasel

all poems by: kyle fasel
www.kylefasel.com
@kylefaselisdead

cover art by: flesh and bone design

photo by: megan leetz

copyright © 2018 kyle fasel
all rights reserved
ISBN-13: 978-1981462629
ISBN-10: 1981462627

dedicated to Tom

You'll always be my best friend, my brother. I'll see you again one day. You'll live in my heart forever.

kyle fasel

nothing memorable
stays the same

the sun will wash out
the vibrant colors
to a dull shade

you'll say I love you
but to a different face
what's dry will be
wet all over again

my younger years
can be found in
empty parking lots
that were once full of
like minded youth
and in houses where
strangers live
that I used to call my home

my roots are covered
by boxes full of thoughts
that hide under dust

I'd like to have a
perfect cinematic
ending to this poem
but
nothing memorable
stays the same.

the clock that watches you sleep
can be thrown against the wall
the minutes will still disappear

the calendar next to the light switch
can be torn to shreds
the days will still eventually
belong to last year

and like the minutes
and like the days
this too will be
behind me
in time

every imperfection
I put in front of my face
sometimes that's all I see

every perfect moment
I push away
sometimes I forget I ever saw them

one day I hope to rearrange
the lines of this poem

my mind is good at

making something small

seem like

the end of the world

the water hits the back of my neck
it begins dropping
to the shower floor

I'm alone
no one to judge me
no one to ask me
why, what, where, when, or who?

a million concerns
spill out of my head
and hit the drain before
the water even does

a place of solitude
can easily become a trap
when you overanalyze like I do

if each one of these concerns
were a drop of water
I'd be drowning

should I learn to swim?
should I learn to be numb?

I should get better
at hiding my concerns from myself
because they will always be here

digging skeletons up
from the bottom
of my closet

throwing them
on my front lawn
for all to see

building a bridge
made of bones
to get past all the demons
that keep running after me

I have a way with
turning on the lights
in a dark crowded room
when no one else can
find the switch

but
when I'm alone
it gets dark again
and the switch disappears

one day
means never.

kyle fasel

I don't want to be
who I used to feel like

my heart was broken and self centered
it took me too long to change
I kept the same old things
and just tried to rearrange

for years
I was running away
from someone

suddenly
hands were gripping tightly
to the bottom of my jeans

I turned around
and realized
it was me

kyle fasel

the families in this town
said their prayers and
laid their heads to rest hours ago

driving eastbound
on an odd numbered street
my headlights are on

but
I feel invisible

empty sidewalks
nobody in sight
perhaps because it's after midnight

I pretend the street lights
are on just for me

and
I feel invisible

a feeling that most find hollow
this is whatI've been longing for

kyle fasel

you won't
see me fall apart
because I keep it
hidden in between
the lines
of my art

exhausted from
focusing
on everything
but me

it's not
a selfless act

just
a distraction
from changing
what I lack

there was nothing there
but in a good way

sorrow was absent
I stared out into the vacancy
it was
dark
empty
and cold
I oddly felt connected

anxiety and overanalyzed thoughts
faded for a few seconds
but it felt like hours

all I needed was nothing
so I could feel again

nothing inspires me

I see a plastic bag
stuck between
the branches of a tree
this image speaks to me

the bag was once freely
blowing in the wind
without a destination
the tree caught the bag
and took away any chance of
further exploration

there are probably details
not mentioned but neither
had any bad intentions

the tree unknowingly
holds back the plastic
bag as it holds on

I suddenly realize what
this image has drawn

me.

if you spent nearly
as much time
doing what
makes you happy
that you spend
making excuses

you would
smile again

kyle fasel

you've let me down
but you've never let me fall

you stare out the window
of your father's house
thoughts as heavy
as the bricks that hold up that home

I'm afraid if your walls could talk
they would say what I don't want to hear
I know you just always pictured things
to be different for yourself

an empty house that smells like smoke
a short temper that gets the best of you
a heart that's bigger than I care to see

I love you

you screamed out
that you hate yourself

I told you
I hated you too

it was the first time
in a long time
that we agreed
on something

if I could see
how it ends
before it starts
would I turn
back around?

every flower
is just a seed
before it sprouts
so beautifully
from the ground

I'm not meant
to know the outcome
before it makes me grow
towards what I don't know

kyle fasel

kicking leaves
off the sidewalk
summer fades
into the past
it takes me back

chicago is painted
orange and red
I'm not trying to
see too far ahead

august turns to fall
and I feel different
leaves change colors as
I change my mind

instead of turning a page
I glance back to read my story
over again
nostalgia still gets the best of me

I feel it hit me
deep down inside
where have the years gone?
are they just hiding from me?

I want to be the same
but I'm different now
time caught up to me
And made me grow

kyle fasel

what I don't know
is making me feel
like somebody else
I change my mind
with the seasons
I'm always searching
for myself

when I'm here
I want to be there
when I'm there
I want to be here
I know that I'm complicated
It's hard to explain what
I keep isolated

don't ever want to be a burden
so I'll keep smiling on the surface

thought I was past this
stronger than this
more self aware
hope it gets better
than this

stitch me up
quickly

so I can
temporarily
move forward

and
permanently
fall backwards

stop looking for what left you
stop looking to replace
start to *rebuild*

you keep trying to mend
the broken and
weathered scraps
it will never be new

you weren't born strong
none of us were

but I've seen you move
more than you remember

I want better for you

rebuild.

kyle fasel

your problems
live in a glass house
without doors

you stare inside
from the front lawn
not able to change
what's yours

two summers after
I didn't go to school anymore

the sun soaked up the stress
of minimum wage
stars reflected off
the windshield of my first car
street lights illuminated
green grass at midnight

that well known
scent of summer
in the suburbs masked
the cigarette smoke

nothing can replace these
youthful thoughts

everything is different now
but
I promise that I'm the same

at least that's
what I tell myself...

kyle fasel

I want to be as happy as my parents
look in these old photos

God knows
it didn't work out for them
but there's
something *beautiful*
about how
they look like
nothing else matters.

don't attempt
to run ahead of fate
it will catch up to you

you're compelling life to move faster
skipping steps when
it's really all about
getting there

the non existent
eternal clock
convinces you
to do what
your parents did when
they were your age

now
mom and dad sit in silence
alone together
loudly overanalyzing
what ifs from the inside
that never get told to anyone

their sentimental thoughts
and regrets are almost identical

now
the only thing mom and dad
know about each other is that
both of them watch the news at 9
with a complete stranger

fate will catch up to you

I love you
but
I don't want to
end up like you

it breaks
my heart
and no one
knows

because
you taught me
how to keep it
all to myself

the hand
that used to feed
is now
a mouth wide open
simply
losing control
of priorities

you burn a bridge and then I build it again

the match in your hand never goes out

stop saying what you want me to hear

spare me the bad news

I've come to terms with despair

I've come to terms with what I fear

I can't say no.

I built a fence made of
second hand selfishness,
last chances, last times
and old wounds.
you hop over it
season after season.

I always break your fall
on the way down.
my heart secretly breaks
in harmony.

kyle fasel

crossing over bridges

my friends burned down years ago

alone in my youth

kyle fasel

I haven't told anybody else
but lately I don't feel like myself

this isn't how I want to be
but I'll stay silent and conceal
what you can't see

anxiety holds my hand
as I overanalyze
what's slipping out of them

did life get hopeless
or did I shift my focus?

I lost my temper when

you lost your way

anger set in when I didn't

know what to say

I've been reading

about unconditional love

and how to open your heart

yet

I continue to exhaust

emotions and reactions

that've proven to make

life fall apart

kyle fasel

I drive past illinois avenue
the houses sit perfectly
I can't see
the problems inside
nor do I want to

Jets to Brazil plays
on the radio
as the moon and
flickering street lights
illuminate off my windshield

for a moment
I pretend everyone I love
is where they want to be
with who they want to
be there with

for a moment
I'm content

when I had nothing
I had it all

a hand-me-down mattress
on a cold basement floor
responsibility didn't haunt me
and no one was keeping score

blankets covered the concrete walls
while I covered my problems
with cigarette smoke

simpler days spent wisely wasting time
it didn't matter that I was broke

there are new locks on that house
but a piece of me still lives there
old memories are under
the new paint on the walls
early morning conversations
still echo through the halls

when I had nothing
I had it all

the sky on my way home
was perfect
it looked like God
replaced it
with a painting
by a famous artist

I thought about
taking a picture
so I could share
the moment with you
but I didn't

I'll keep that memory
just for me

it's okay to keep
some things
to myself

when I'm uninspired,
I'm lost.

when I'm lost,
I'm inspired.

watching it all
slowly dissolve
is worse than
it all suddenly
destructing
in seconds

there's too much
time to hope
that it will all
turn around

call me a realist
or whatever
you prefer
but if something
will soon
be nothing
just destroy it
right now

falling backwards onto
sentimental thoughts
is simpler than thinking
right now

because we don't have
to wait and wonder how

kyle fasel

I see skin
you see stone

I blame the days
I was a boy left all alone
nobody told me
what was right
or what was wrong
I can still see myself
innocently running
across my neighbor's lawn
grass stains on my hands and knees
trying to make sense of anything

I never wanted
to be like stone
I blame the days
I was a boy left all alone

my worries
hold my head under water

scared
 helpless
  and cold

I oddly find solace
in **the silence**
right before I run
out of breath
the worries pull me
above the water

wet clothes
 blue face
  and coughing up a lung

and all I can think about is
the silence

kyle fasel

when
you were running
down the street
that's when I knew
I loved you

after
you moved far away
that's when I knew
I lost you

and that I'll never stop
loving you

years after
you left my life
I realized you
were only there to
help me grow

kyle fasel

you asked me

"what do you do
for the rest of your life
when you realize
you don't like anything?"

and that's when I knew
we were one in the same

44

kids stay home from school
the yellow buses are parked
and painted white
an unexplainable and youthful feeling
of escape is restless

it's under appreciated
in the moment
but when they're adults
they'll long for
what they feel today

kyle fasel

stop taking what doesn't belong to you
and making it your problem
up late
        tossing
                turning
                        and contemplating
tomorrow has worries of its own

find hope in letting life play out
whether you worry or not
it'll end the same way

when in doubt
remember how it all worked out
it pulled you down before you got up

kyle fasel

talk talk talk
all about what you're GOING to do

talk talk talk
all about who you're GOING to be

talk talk talk
that's all it is

prove me wrong

I hold out
an open hand
to help

but it keeps getting
mistaken
for

a swinging fist
ready to harm
something
good

kyle fasel

when it's in my reach
it's standard

when it's gone for good
it's extraordinary

endlessly romanticizing what
I can't get back

don't let
who you love
take you away from
what you love

and

don't let
what you love
take you away from
who you love

balance keeps love strong

kyle fasel

in high school
weakness seemed
to cover me like

well...

like a confused kid
in high school

that had so much
to
learn
feel
and get over

now I look back
and say none of it
was really that bad

in ten years
I want to look
back on today
and say the same

I washed my face
looked up quickly
and glanced
in the mirror

it must have been months
since I took a
good look at myself

I stood and stared
at my reflection
like a deer in headlights

my face told a story
better than these words
ever could

go
work a job
that makes you feel hollow
so you can
make money to buy things
you don't really need

go
buy a big house to fill with
the things you don't really need

go
buy an overpriced car
and show it off to
people that don't really care

go
spend all your time working
instead of pursuing
what makes you happy

the front door of that big house
is a trap
the employees only door at work
is a trap
the driver's side door of that new car
is a trap

The American Dream

kyle fasel

when you go out of your way
to show how much you don't care

      it shows me that you actually do care

      more than you want to admit...

kyle fasel

I've pulled flowers
from the dirt
confusing them
with weeds
after it was
too late

uncertainty is
spilling all over me
from a glass
filled too high

my thoughts race
as my body stays
in the exact same
place

time stands still
and
I wish so badly
it was a metaphor
but
I'm literally stuck
in this moment

kyle fasel

I hit
the side of the TV
to make the blurry lines fade away
it only makes it worse

my solutions keep making
it all worse

I press
the power button
so I can turn the problem off
instead of solving it
this feels all too familiar

The TV stays on
as if there was no attempt
of interruption

I finally unplug the TV
from the wall
but it somehow stays on
giving off just enough light
so I can't fall asleep

comfort made you
stand still longer
than you intended to
it was the easiest way to maintain
now everything's the same

days blur together
what once was enjoyable
is now an inconvenience
'I love you'
has shifted from a feeling
to what you're supposed to say

ironically
that comfort was the seed
of you
now being uncomfortable
unmotivated
and stuck here

are you afraid of losing comfort?
or
are you afraid of change?

I'm afraid of you feeling comfortable

kyle fasel

we're so focused on

washing the blood off our hands

that we never realize it's actually our own

been feeling low
I can't see why
whenever a good reason
gets too close
I cover my eyes with pride

I thought I was
better than this
stronger than this
more self aware

appearing to be
made of stone
hoping the ones
that lean on me
are delusional to
the fact that I'm really
just skin and bones

what you don't know
won't hurt you
but what happens when
what you don't know
makes you feel like
somebody else?

I whisper anxiously
to my emotions to
keep quiet and
stay inside

and the story continues...

kyle fasel

the letters
are already here

the shapes
are already here

waiting
on
you

to make them your own

kyle fasel

solitude is
my drug of choice

but like anything else

an excess amount
of it

can destroy me

kyle fasel

the truth is
I'm weak

my skinny arms
are as strong
as they appear
not to be

I can't build
the strength
to bring up
emotions
from deep down
inside of me

kyle fasel

do the readers
know the story
better than the authors?

because the last page
of my story
was torn out
and everyone
remembers it
except for me

I'm lost
but I'd rather be lost
than stand still

I don't really miss anyone
    I miss the days and the nights
        I spent with them

I sit in a crowded room
I want nothing more than
to be like
the off-white paint on these walls
unnoticed and ordinary

days later
I sit in an empty room
chipping away
this off-white paint
that covers me

kyle fasel

I care about you
more than I want to

in ten years will you be
where I wish you were
right now?

your silence
screams to me
that you won't
be

but as long as
you're happy...

kyle fasel

it's hard to remember today
when all you think about is yesterday
there's a feeling in my bones
that if I keep staring behind me
I'll end up all alone

I'm
lying on the living room floor
STILL
worrying about falling down

it's
sunny and 65 degrees outside
yet there's
STILL
clouds hovering in my mind

years of growth have passed
and I'm
STILL
creating fear from the inside

if you're never
going to forget
at least forgive

but do it soon
because
forgiveness
is fading

my friends
family
and strangers
have resorted to
blaming
    and blaming
        and blaming

once forgiveness
has completely
faded away

I won't feel at home
anymore
in this world
that's gone astray

kyle fasel

so quick to
raise your fist
cover your ears
open your mouth
and resist

from your hypocritical
point of view
it's either night or day
black or white
you don't see gray
unless someone agrees
with every single word
you say

how's it feel to know it all?
how's it feel to know you
stand on the knowledge
to never fall?

I'm crossing my fingers
that it'll cross your mind
to value
other opinions
and recognize when
to just listen

a wrong turn
can still
lead you home

kyle fasel

it's safe to say
I never
thought you'd
fall
from
the tree

would it have been different
if you opened up to me?

I can only read
what's on
your skin
to see

don't take this the wrong way
it sounds trite and cliché

but I want you
to be who
you used
to be

strange how
it's harder to let go
after you find out
they were never
holding back

and we
wonder why
we always
end up here

we lose the details
in this instant age
we want it all right now
even if it's filtered or fake

no time to look back
and read over the page
because we're
mindlessly staring at
shifting the blame
and counterfeit smiles
on display

false views of insecurity
disguised as reality

trivial things

fear is an
excuse for
when it's
easier
to stand still

fear isn't
in the way

your tolerance
for it is

if they never made it complicated
if they never made you feel blue
if they never made you cry
if they never kept you up
if they never disagreed

was it really even
love?

if they always made it seem so simple
if they always made you glow bright
if they always made you smile
if they always let you rest
if they always agreed

was it really even
love?

always worried
always consuming
myself in what others think

am I happy with the person
that reflects in the mirror?
this old shirt
the same old shoes
and the same blue eyes
a little more faded
but the same

I turn around
I don't see a judge and a jury
it's all in my head
so why live like I'm on trial?

am I happy with the person
that reflects in the mirror?
this old pair of blue jeans
the same old records
and the same half opened smile
a little more faded
but the same

stop worrying
stop consuming yourself in what others think

I need to take my own advice

kyle fasel

what I don't say
is what really haunts me

years of unseen thoughts
hidden behind uncertainty
disguised as confidence

sooner or later I might
convince myself that
I never had anything
to say

kyle fasel

I turn the record over

but the same song

still plays

kyle fasel

you can't
reach your goal
by simply creating it
in your mind

if that was the case
there would be more
fulfilled hearts, happiness
and purpose

but instead
there's more
wasted potential, regret
and hidden half empty dreams

thinking of a goal, pursuing it
and getting to the finish line
carries a great distance in between

I'm afraid some of us are
too busy making excuses
to go the distance

stop making excuses

kyle fasel

a glimpse at death can bring
a soul back to life

it's unfortunate that
some people have to
nearly touch heaven or hell
to start living again

82

kyle fasel

there's a difference
between
being ungrateful
and wanting more

I can't decide which one
I'm feeling right now

you're not always on my side
but everyone around here
keeps telling me that you are
it's just hard to believe sometimes
alright?

you keep moving
I stay right where I've always been
you move faster and faster and faster
I slow down

I'll admit that I'm a little bitter towards you
more than I even care to mention

you've taken away loved ones
you've made me feel hollow
you've ripped me open

and

you've made me feel whole
you've helped me find solace in
places I didn't know it existed
most importantly
you've healed my wounds

time heals.

you were in love
and he was in denial

the shoes that
used to fit so well
are too big now

the house that saw you
grow from old to young again
has different locks on the doors

the money that made you secure
is in someone else's pockets

the hand that used to feed is
now a mouth wide open

there's a crack in the door
instead of opening it up
I stand still and stare at how
imperfect it is

I know I should just walk past it

but I'm a hypocrite

the truth that
tore you down
made you change
for the best

the truth can
hurt you

but eventually
it will
heal you

the wounds are
temporary

your actions are
permanent

kyle fasel

"I can't"
is the cop-out
that's stealing
my

satisfaction
happiness
motivation
self-worth
progress
purpose
and
_____ away

I play
the victim
but
deep
deep
down
inside
I know
that
I'm the thief

I can't

bury the memories

because

I'm too weak

to dig the grave

or maybe

it's because

love is stronger

than

my selfish ways

the stars shine brighter
for me than the daylight ever has
headlights echo off the windows
and I feel at home

hiding from the sunrise
because when everyone's asleep
I don't have to compromise
a lack of lights shows me
how disconnected I can be

every bulb is burnt out
and it's alright

I can still see vividly

impatience can create desperation

that doesn't even exist

it's like waking up from a nightmare

and believing that it really happened

fate won't forget your name

if you stop

and at least try to enjoy the moment

don't let the future break you

into a thousand pieces

like the past does to me

wish you could
meet me halfway
it's unfair for me
to carry all the weight

if you only
knew how it feels
to be left alone
and figure it out
on your own

I was always there
for you when you
couldn't follow through

I was the key
under the welcome mat
in front of the house
only a priority when
plans didn't work out

give me what I want
and eventually
I'll be unsatisfied

oh
what a heartless mind
this body unknowingly
holds

I'm ungrateful
and problem causing
I'm broken
and can't be fixed

and yes
I'll keep breaking
eventually beyond repair

love is mistaken
for control
when you lose
the strength
to figure it out
on your own

kyle fasel

you locked my concern
outside in the cold

meanwhile
you were shivering inside
longing for someone
to take hold

if I didn't care about you
I wouldn't still be out here

but you clearly can't see that
or maybe you just don't want to

for half of my life
I thought I was made to
open my heart and
say what comes to mind

but
lately I can't stop pushing
what I want and need aside

procrastinating
like it'll be written
on my gravestone

sadly
it appears to be
what I do best when
I'm all alone

holding our troubles

high above my head

is easier than

holding my tongue

kyle fasel

overthinking is
like raindrops
hitting the rooftop
in the middle
of the night

it keeps me awake
yet in the morning
it is all dried up
and life is still
the same

kyle fasel

permanence might fade
this life blooms then wilts away
take risks while you can

your honest smile is behind

the morning clouds

your selfless ways are behind

the midnight stars

I can't see you

but I believe that you're up there

I wanted to let you know that we're still

falling

     apart

         down

            here

               without

                  y

                    o

                      u

kyle fasel

thunder clashes far off in the distance
I immediately run for cover
as if a storm has painted the sky
from blue to black

I believe what I hear
more than what I can see

I have such little faith in my strength
that I have the same reaction to
trivial things
and death creeping up behind me

when did I become so afraid of
everything?

to change
you must let go

for your flaw filled hands
can only hold on to so much

and you will gain control from losing

and life will continue to prove that it isn't
how we thought it would be

kyle fasel

we're not the only authors

of our lives

the pen is in other people's hands

more than we know

and I think that's okay

if the beginning, the middle

and the end

was solely written by us

life would be too predictable

kyle fasel

the tall grass sways in the midwestern breeze
every piece in harmony

growing together
whether they're surrounded by
gray snow or dead leaves

growing together
whether they're brightened by
the summer sun or street lights in the distance

no matter the circumstance
they'll never leave
the ones beside them

it's admirable
really

this is what nature has that humans have lost
or maybe we never even had it

I hope to God
I have it

have faith in fate
it will change
what your words
never can

don't always
open your mouth
in the moment

learn to
silently open your eyes
to what lies ahead

kyle fasel

there's a thorn in your rib cage
thank God it's too short to reach your heart

you need to pull it out from your side,
heal and learn from your scars

but you don't have the guts
to go back to the start

when we're in a crisis
we're vulnerable, regretful
and more willing
to mend whatever
will allow us to breathe again

some of us pray to God
some of us make promises
for a better tomorrow

but for a lot of us
it takes that crisis
to make us stop like
a deer in headlights

it shouldn't take lies
to bring honesty out

it shouldn't take a house fire
to prevent the flame from
hitting the floor

kyle fasel

second chances

were the first thing

you thought about

kyle fasel

in the morning
and under the moon
I dig up nostalgic days
that were buried by
the hands of a clock

I endlessly
compare and stare at these
younger, simpler,
ignorant, yet innocent
moments in time

if only
just one of these
old pictures
in my dirty hands
would come to life
and be the here and now again

then I could drop
this shovel for good
and finally escape
today for yesterday

just like I've always
wanted to

kyle fasel

feels like I've been
screaming into a
broken payphone
in the middle of a field

you're acting
like I've been
opening my mouth without
allowing any words to fall out

am I a book
with the middle part ripped out?

am I a crown
without a king or queen?

am I a reply
without a request?

am I a ghost town
full of people?

am I a consequence
without an action?

am I a broken bone
in a perfect world?

no.

I'm just misunderstood by you

kyle fasel

I can't stop foreshadowing to a near future
where there's even more distance between us

the even more part scares me the most

I don't mean to be negative here
I'm really trying
I swear
I've even been avoiding the rain
and situations that are out of my control

it's just that with time comes age
and with age comes distance
from our youth and we're not getting
any younger

we've been proving this to be true
for a while now

I know you haven't necessarily felt us drift apart
but I'm sure you'll realize it later
rather than sooner

basically
all I'm trying to say
is that I miss the simple days
when we were killing time
to get here

dear you,

there's a purpose
for all of this
the smiles
the letdowns
every decision
every last kiss

when life suddenly
seems to fall apart
it's beginning to
peacefully write
another chapter
at the exact same time
the end is a new start

the meaning lives
in the hellos
and the goodbyes
it's all intertwined
we just have to stop
always asking why

kyle fasel

I had to give up
to finally get what I deserved
or what I had coming to me

'everything happens for a reason'
echoed from my head down to my heart

fate connected the disconnected
as I knew it would

my negativity was just
getting the best of me
in this trying moment

the sorrow and the silence
now made sense
lonely nights surrounded by no one
and what I falsely saw as nothing
spoke volumes for once

the pain was the water and the sun
I was the wilting flower all along
now I bloom with appreciation
to what forced me to grow again

kyle fasel

it takes us losing
something
someone
ourselves
or time
to truly
appreciate
what we once
took for granted

I don't want loss
to be the
eye opening moment
anymore

why are we so
blind to good things?

115

kyle fasel

we acknowledged the scars
of a lonely past

and held hands
gazing into the future

yeah
I know
something's got to change
but it's easier to just stand here
and lose faith

I could blame
mom and dad
and say it's a
hand-me-down reaction
or lack thereof

but excuses aren't for me anymore

I wish
the wind didn't blow so cold
so we could go for a walk
but it's okay
because
the way you look at me
warms something inside of me

and I wish
it was the 4th of July
so we could watch the fireworks
but it's okay
because
the way you make me feel
sparks something bright inside of me

and I wish
I had all the answers
so I could always be right
but it's okay
because
the way I hold you in my arms
always feels right

kyle fasel

you sleep with the moon
     I stay up finding hope
          under the street lights

kyle fasel

today is the same as
yesterday

can't tell if I'm
feeling dizzy
from routine
or
from being sentimental
it's one of the two
or both

eventually
has been my answer to
most questions
lately

yet when I put things aside
it means more time
running in
circles

will I ever
stop feeling dizzy?

eventually

kyle fasel

silence calms me

silence scares me

silence builds me

silence breaks me

silence saves me

silence is always there

silence is never there

silence speaks to me

I want to talk to the person
I used to be

innocent
ignorant
and
arrogant

back then if I knew
what I know now
maybe I'd be down-and-out
instead of getting better

maybe I'd be holding on to
what let me go
instead of rebuilding

we aren't supposed to know
the next chapter without
reading the ones before it

kyle fasel

you notice your shadow
but ignore the light that
makes it possible

your eyes have adjusted
to the dark

and I hope over time
you will see life differently

the year was 1998.
the cream-colored phone cord
extended like a tightrope
from the kitchen,
down five stairs
to the closed basement door.

little did I know
that the dream of
a flawless suburban family
tried to walk that tightrope
of a phone cord.
It fell right off
and it never attempted to get back up.

my mom stood behind the basement door.
the phone was in her shaky hands.
she was in tears and disbelief.

when she opened the door,
our lives were changed forever.

I was too young
to understand it then,
but that was the first time
I was exposed to reality.

it was my introduction to
being let down.

kyle fasel

wanting more than you have
can get the best of you

staring into the future
can get the best of you

don't discredit the present
because the best of you
may be right here
in this moment

it's never taken

a thief stealing what's yours

to lock the doors at night

so

why do you only think of solutions

to prevent every problem

after it's too late?

my quiet
   time and place

is when and where

it's the loudest
   inside my head

sure
I'm alone
   with my thoughts

but the what ifs
   are keeping me company

kyle fasel

growing tired of
being the problem solver
wherever my heart decides to stay

growing tired of
saying "I'm so sorry"
when I shouldn't have the first word to say

the walls inside of me made of heartbreak
never seem to go away

I wonder why...

kyle fasel

a wounded heart

doesn't want

to hear

an optimistic mouth

stray the sadness away

a wounded heart

doesn't want

a loving hand

trying to heal

what only time can

a wounded heart

simply wants

a shoulder to cry on

kyle fasel

early in the morning

I ask myself questions

that kept me up late

the night before

today and tomorrow
will one day be
nostalgic memories
I reminisce about

they will somehow
make me resent the present

it's a state of mind I know
all too well
I don't think
I can make it stop

but honestly
I don't want it to

sometimes
I wish I wasn't an artist
so I could just let go of
what I really want to do.

is there an easier way out of here?

I could follow in the footsteps
of people that always lived to
satisfy their parents and society.

go work a job I hate,
come home, eat dinner, watch TV,
sleep next to a person I don't love anymore,
retire at sixty-five,
complain out of boredom for about ten years
and then die.

actually,
never mind.

my heart's broken?
I miss the way it used to be?
getting older scares me?

they've all been said before
they don't compare to my current emotions
my thoughts are heavy, broken and scattered
on the floor

when you took your last breath
this place faded from a home
to just a house
it's not the same after your left

I still hear you walking down the stairs
I still see you sleeping with the TV on

I distract my sadness and
say you're in a better place
no matter what
my heart still breaks

please just stay a little longer
we can smile and wipe away the tears
sit in the living room
and reminisce on past years
please just stay a little longer

church bells ring
as I straighten my tie
there's a hole in my chest
memories of you in my mind

this isn't goodbye
this is *see you soon*

kyle fasel

romanticizing time I'll never get back
I'm blind to the anxiety
that used to cover my optimistic eyes

I only think of when
shooting stars fell back then

but what about when I fell
and no one was there to catch me?

I continue to romanticize time
spent out of place

nostalgia lies
and tells me that I had a smile on my face

I'd rather pretend that life was better yesterday
than be honest
and say a lot is still the same today

kyle fasel

my front lawn
is lined with headstones.

nobody's resting under there,
just memories of a distant past.

I'm lying flowers down,
mourning time I'll never get back.

kyle fasel

I don't know who I am anymore. I sit up at night and wonder who I miss. I wonder what I miss. In between the late night TV I'm not paying attention to, I wonder if I really miss anything or anyone at all. I'm in a weird spot. It sounds scary but it's really not. I think this is all a growing pain. I'm not sure what it's growing towards...but it's something.

kyle fasel

if I were to open my chest

I could feel weightless

from your love

but my arms are crossed

blocking out

your grace

you constantly display
what you hold close

are you confident or do
you constantly
need to be reassured
you're holding the
right things close?

a broken clock stands
on the shelf
it reminds me that
our lives stopped
when yours ended

even though you're gone
I swear we'll
remember you

I said goodbye
without regret

now
every sunday
I think about our
time together that
I'll never forget

Kyle Fasel lives in Orland Park, Illinois. He plays bass guitar in the band Real Friends. This is his first book. He's also written, performed and recorded many pieces of spoken word poetry.

Made in the USA
Monee, IL
02 December 2019

17765795R00085